JOSHUA and the Fall of Jericho

Numbers 27:12–23 and Joshua 1–3; 5:13–6:27 for children

Sara H. Low

Illustrated by Mina Price

CONCORDIA PUBLISHING HOUSE · SAINT LOUIS

Moses climbed a mountain and saw the Promised Land.
Then, on Joshua, son of Nun, he firmly placed his hands.
Moses gave authority to Joshua that day,
Trusting him to wisely lead the people, come what may.

As Moses' right-hand man, he was poised to lead the way.
He listened very carefully to all God had to say:
"Be strong and courageous. Step out in faith and go
To the land I promised you a long, long time ago."

Obeying God's command, Joshua began to plan.
He sent two spies to Jericho to inspect the land.
The spies were almost caught by the king of Jericho,
But Rahab hid them on her roof and later let them go.

Rahab was a woman who knew God's power and might.
She asked the spies for kindness for saving them that night.
The men agreed to Rahab's plan: a scarlet cord she tied
To her window as a sign to save all those inside.

Nearer still to Jericho, Joshua saw a man
Standing right in front of him, a sword drawn in His hand.
Joshua inquired, "Are You for us or against?"
When he heard the answer, he fell in reverence.

"The army of the Lord is under My command.
Take off your sandals now, for on holy ground you stand."
And though the Lord's commander was not on either side,
He strengthened Joshua for the battle that was drawing nigh.

In the walls of Jericho, the gates were shut up tight
Because the people were afraid of the Israelites.
So what do you think Joshua chose to do that day?
Again, he listened carefully to all God had to say:

"Jericho, its king and men, I've placed into your hand.
Follow My instructions for how to win the land.
March around the city once, and do this for six days.
But on the seventh, you will march in a different way."

"The priests will march in front of all, carrying the ark
And blowing on their trumpets as the group embarks.
Wait until the seventh day to shout and make some noise;
Have the army join the blast and loudly lift their voice.

"Then, the walls of Jericho will crumble, tumble down.
The troops can then go straight in right from level ground."
Joshua told the people the instructions from the Lord.
They listened and obeyed their leader at his word.

The priests, with their trumpets, went before God's holy ark.
Soldiers went in front and back, and all began to march.
They marched around the city once. Next day, they did the same.
They did this for six days until the seventh finally came.

They marched around seven times, and with the trumpet blast
And great big shouts from Israel, the giant walls collapsed!
Rumble! Rumble! Crash! Crash! The walls could not withstand
Israel's obedience and God's mighty hand.

The men rushed in the city and destroyed it with the sword,
Every house except the one that had the scarlet cord.
The same two spies whom Rahab hid went back into her place,
Brought her and her family out, and showed them God's great grace.

Just as Joshua listened and obeyed,
Jesus, too, heard carefully all God had to say.
He spoke what His Father told Him; His words were always true.
He obeyed His Father and died for me and you.

We, too, can listen carefully to all God has to say.
Open up your Bible and read it every day!
When times get tough, do not doubt instructions from the Lord.
Every day, trust and obey our Savior at His word.

Dear Parent,

The wall around Jericho was an impressive human construction. It was fourteen feet thick and thirty-five feet tall. It was impenetrable, and that's why Jericho stood against its enemies for hundreds of years. Joshua's army could try to tunnel through it or pile up earth to build a ramp over it. Either option would have taken months and left them exposed to their opponent's army. But in this dramatic story, God's people defeated Jericho in just seven days without a shovel or axe or arrow. They used their voices and trumpets to create a cacophonous assault. And God caused the wall to crumble before everyone's eyes.

Children love to hear this story because it's fantastical. It's also one of those Bible accounts that secular historians say is myth. Those who believe God's Word, however, understand that this true event shows us that God will judge humankind and will punish the unrighteous. The story doesn't end there, of course.

God's way is vastly different from man's. Joshua, his army, and Rahab and her family were saved by faith. Joshua obeyed God's directions because he had faith. God kept His promise to deliver the children of Israel to the Promised Land, and He will keep His promise to deliver us to eternal life with Him through Jesus' work on the cross for us.

The editor